GARDEN
CLUBS & SPADES

THE AUTHOR
HAS ALSO WRITTEN

PEOPLE OF NOTE

A SCORE OF SYMPHONY FACES

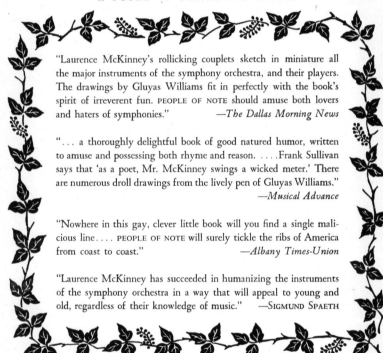

"Laurence McKinney's rollicking couplets sketch in miniature all the major instruments of the symphony orchestra, and their players. The drawings by Gluyas Williams fit in perfectly with the book's spirit of irreverent fun. PEOPLE OF NOTE should amuse both lovers and haters of symphonies." —*The Dallas Morning News*

". . . a thoroughly delightful book of good natured humor, written to amuse and possessing both rhyme and reason. . . . .Frank Sullivan says that 'as a poet, Mr. McKinney swings a wicked meter.' There are numerous droll drawings from the lively pen of Gluyas Williams." —*Musical Advance*

"Nowhere in this gay, clever little book will you find a single malicious line. . . . PEOPLE OF NOTE will surely tickle the ribs of America from coast to coast." —*Albany Times-Union*

"Laurence McKinney has succeeded in humanizing the instruments of the symphony orchestra in a way that will appeal to young and old, regardless of their knowledge of music." —SIGMUND SPAETH

Published by E. P. DUTTON & CO., Inc.

GARDEN CLUBS & SPADES

BY

LAURENCE McKINNEY

PICTURES BY

HELEN E. HOKINSON

1941

NEW YORK

E. P. DUTTON & CO., INC.

ACKNOWLEDGMENTS

Acknowledgement is made to *Harper's Magazine, Life,* and the *New York Herald Tribune* for permission to reprint some of the verses and articles.

Special thanks also is due *The New Yorker* for giving permission to use the drawings in this book by Helen E. Hokinson. These appeared originally in *The New Yorker.* Likewise to Phyllis McGinley Hayden for her kindness in lending an original Hokinson drawing.

The proper names in this book mostly refer to varieties of flowers. There are others which I hope are imaginary and others too well known to explain about. If people will name roses after Presidents, other people's wives, or whatever comes into their minds at the time, I don't feel even vicariously guilty. They also name flowers after themselves which accounts for a lot of funny names, too. But in any case here are apologies wherever apologies are due.

THE AUTHOR

TO GARDEN PESTS

WITHOUT WHOSE
INDOMITABLE PERSEVERANCE
INSATIABLE APPETITE, AND
FONDNESS FOR LARGE FAMILIES,
MILLIONS OF EMBATTLED WOMEN
WOULD NOT BE ON THEIR KNEES
THESE DAYS
INDUCING GROWTH
PRODUCING BEAUTY, AND
REDUCING WAISTLINES, AND
I WOULD HAVE NEITHER
A HAPPY SUBJECT, NOR
A POSSIBLE MARKET
FOR THIS BOOK.

GARDEN
CLUBS & SPADES

CONTENTS AND LIST OF ILLUSTRATIONS

(Illustrations are in Italics)

"Good Morning, little Morning Glories."

IN THE BEGINNING

The Garden Club of Eden
                            was the first that history shows,
   Which Adam and his Madam can attest,
From a simple cotyledon
                            she created all her clothes
   And the Devil was the only garden pest.
When they had no luck with apples
                            they went out and turned the key
   And engaged in raising Cain, with sinking heart,
So the modern girl who grapples
                            with a garden ought to see
   That gardens have been failures from the start.

You transplant it with a dibble
                            and the cutworm starts to nibble,
   And it's always much too dry, wet, cold or hot,
And no matter what you *will* do,
                            things will die of moles or mildew —
   "OH! a garden is a lovesome thing, God wot! !"

Nowadays your muscles harden
                    as you daily tend your phlox
    On the border where you've knelt and watched and
                                                    sprayed
Where you found your little garden
                    was a parking lot for rocks
    And there's not a decent name you'd call a spade
Where the scent of fertilizer
                    is the one that greets your nose
    And there's much too much of mulching all the
                                                    while,
Where the rose-bug, sly and wiser,
                    always beats you to a rose,
    And when e'er you mention cynoglossum, Smile!

Dig and dust and prune and sprinkle,
                    try each gadget, learn each wrinkle,
    And you'll get one pink petunia, like as not,
For the silly game makes fools of
                    all but those you buy your tools of,—
    "OH! a garden is a lovesome thing, God wot! !"

GARDEN ALMANAC
OR MULCH ADO ABOUT NOTHING

In her garden
Phoebe Fox
Grows phlox
And hollyhocks.

Jan. —Feb.

In the days of ice and snow
   Donning overcoat and rubbers
Phoebe Fox will gaily go
   And gather with the Garden Clubbers.
Gentlemen — for modest fees —
   Monthly make the members wiser
In the art of pruning trees —
Growing lawns, and peonies,
Mealy bugs, and things like these —
   And the use of fertilizer.
      Once a man who looked like Gable
      Showed them how to set a table —
Things a gardener should know.

Mar. —Apr.

In the early spring appear
   Pussy willows, mud, and peepers,
And those catalogs from Dreer,
   Sutton, Totty, Burpee, Scheepers;
List of triple-tested seeds,
   Makes of sturdy trowels and dibbles —

"I think I'll order some baby's breath to put"

Funny forks for teasing weeds,
Sprinklers of a dozen speeds,
Pots — and those alluring feeds
     That a stealthy cutworm nibbles.
          And a handy thing to try on
          That rebellious dandelion —
Phoebe buys them every year.

May — Jun.

In the mulching month of May
     Phoebe works, no one can doubt it,
On her knees the livelong day,
     Makes her bed and lies about it:
"Here's alyssum in a row —
     Here is where my lovely flax is —
This is where my lilies grow —
See, my cosmos starts to show —
Nothing's very sure, you know
     Only baby's breath and taxus."
          Platycodon, physostegia,
          Ageratum, aquilegia,
Hopefully the markers say.

Jul. — Aug.

But in her garden
Phoebe Fox
Grows phlox
And hollyhocks.

"I'm so angry with the maples."

It was Mrs. Aaron Ward who started it. She had listened in at a Garden Club meeting in the house and although she admitted being potted at the time immediately circulated the idea of a *Garden* Garden Club. They held their organization meeting over by the fence, a spot to which Dorothy Perkins was particularly attached. Miss Lingard and Mrs. Jenkins came from across the border purposely to be there, Mrs. Perry arrived early and Clara Butt finally showed up bringing with her the Reverend H. Ewbank, who, being the only man present, was both honored and embarrassed.

"First, somebody should read the minutes," announced Mrs. Aaron Ward, with authority. Clara Butt, who was the tallest, took a look at the sundial and reported, "Twenty after three." A motion was immediately made to dispense with them, which was the correct thing to do, according to Mrs. Aaron Ward.

"I move we have the Report of the Standing Committees," said Mrs. Jenkins, brightly.

"I move we dispense with them, too," said Miss Lingard who had come out before Mrs. Jenkins and disliked being pointedly called Miss, without even a first name.

"If you dispense with committees, my dear," said

"We raised it from one of the canary's seeds."

Mrs. Aaron Ward, "you dispense with Garden Clubs. Mrs. Perry, will you give your report on Garden Pests?"

Mrs. Perry began rather stiffly. "There are two main kinds of pests," she said, "the two-legged and the four-legged. These are again subdivided into those who bite, those who trample, and those who make cracks."

The Reverend H. Ewbank nodded slightly. "As for instance?" he asked, encouragingly.

"Well, there's the Bad Minton Bug, which tramples, and the Golf Bug, which swings at you," began Mrs. Perry. "Then there's the Pic Nic, or Outdoor Mealy Bug. They appear in the summer. Rain drives them away but otherwise they attract ants and spread desolation. They are the Two-legged Type. Then there's the Cocktail Hound."

"Four-legged?" asked the Reverend H. Ewbank.

"Two, and a sucking type," said Mrs. Perry. "They come in great hordes, swarm for a while and then completely disappear. They are found with the two High Executioners, High Balls and High Heels. High Balls spray alcohol on you; High Heels make a hole in one."

"Must be related to the Golf Bug," said the Reverend H. Ewbank. Mrs. Perry went on. "The last is the Seven Year Nuisance, a picking type." She subsided.

"That's very good, Mrs. Perry," said Mrs. Aaron Ward. "Now, Mrs. Jenkins, will you report for the Committee on Food?"

Mrs. Jenkins to Miss Lingard's evident pleasure was totally unprepared. "Let's," she said, gaily, "just talk about what each of us likes best."

"Well, so far as I am concerned," said Mrs. Aaron Ward, "Give me plenty of well-rotted —"

"Does that account for your unusual complexion?" asked Dorothy Perkins.

"That's just a new spray I'm using, nothing I'm fed," replied Mrs. Aaron Ward. "But you look in the pink yourself, how do you manage it?"

"Well," said Dorothy Perkins, "I've been hanging around here a long time and I've seen a lot of new diets — things that come from bones or cans. But as you have said I think we all feel that there is nothing so nourishing as well-rotted —"

"I don't," said Clara Butt. "It burns me up the way it is used around here."

"You're probably slightly acid anyway, dear," said Mrs. Jenkins. "I admit I was brought up the old-fashioned way. Topsoil and leaf-mold were good enough for me. These new test-tube babies rather appall me. Some of them are so weak that they have to use iron to get them to stand up."

Mrs. Aaron Ward had run out of ideas. "We should really have a lot of committees if we want to be a real garden club," she apologized. "And I think at this meeting we should pick delegates."

"What are delegates?" asked the Reverend H. Ewbank.

"They are a sort of Annual Rambler," replied Mrs. Aaron Ward, "And now for tea — hybrid of course."

But the Reverend H. Ewbank had lost interest now that he couldn't ask any more questions. He turned and signalled his companion.

"Come, Clara Butt," he said, "I think that it is time that we two went back to bed."

SPRING FLORA

Written in, and / or, during Depression

The Annual Reports are out,
    The Early Proxy lifts its head,
We push the printed leaves aside,
And see, with fast declining pride,
    The Balance burgeoning with red.

But wealth we buried in the ground,
    Forgot about, and left unseen,
Returns our interest many fold:
The Crocuses are lined with gold,
    The Jonquil spikes are long and green.

*"You know what I like about these gardens is
no cutworms."*

TRUDGING THROUGH
THE TULIPS

Every year Grand Central Palace
Is the host for hemerocallis,
Antirrhinum, amaryllis, scabiosa, salpiglossis,
Where Manhattan and the Missus
Can bone up about narcissus
And can mingle, elbows touching, with the cultured
    upper classes.

Where until their footsteps falter
They can thrill to Stumpp and Walter
And can totter through the Totty's and the things that
    Max can Schling,
Scenes transplanted, pot and parcel,
May be tough on metatarsal
But are what the penthouse planters wouldn't miss for
    anything.

Here's a quiet spot that yester-
Day was growing in Westchester
Now it blooms an Eve-less Eden where the Bronx and
    Brooklyn meet,

"Come, Marie, you smelled those before."

In the shadow of the Waldorf
Social strata have been called off
And the human race awarded to the most enduring feet.

Doses for each garden malady,
Lunches, rather vague and salady,
Endless garden club exhibits rendered chaste by tireless
    toil,
Catalogs and tools appalling
They discover, arches falling,
As they mingle with the tillers and the ticklers of the
    soil.

For this Chromium Gomorrah
Likes its prisoned floors of flora
Where the sight of rows of roses and of orchids over-
    whelms,
Fie upon that strife fomenter
Who, at Rockefeller Center,
Smiles upon a man-made forest and its lonely, lonely
    elms.

"Won't you please give first prize to Mrs. Gleason?
She's going to have a baby."

Mother dear, I'd rather not
Pass upon your "mossy grot,"
Let me judge another day
When you've learned a better way.
Surely, Mother, you must know
Not a decent Flower Show
Would exhibit such distortion
Of the standards of proportion.
Mother, you don't know, it seems,
Anything of color schemes,
No distinction can I see,
Nor originality,
Take that "brooklet," why it could
Be observed in *any* wood,
And to show it can't be right
Not a Chinese thing's in sight.
Mother Nature, why, oh! why,
CAN'T you learn from Constance Spry?

"It's something from California. I'm not sure"

Helen E. Hokinson

"Sword Lilies," I told the Florist,
　　"Show how those sharp words of hers
Left my heart a murky forest.
　　Coming as my messengers
They will say with grief she's filled me
　　Leaving me for other lads;
Send her sadness." But he billed me:
　　One Dozen Glads.

"Golden balls of Autumn's splendor
　　Speak the words I'm thinking of.
Send them, Florist, and you send her
　　Passioned sentiments of love.
Let them have no weak or thin voice
　　But with crash of brass or drums
Let Love shriek." I got the invoice:
　　One Dozen Mums.

*"And right here under the peonies, I'm sure I
saw a fairy."*

MY GARDEN

"Let's have a garden," I said to my wife.
 "My dear," she replied, "I would simply love it —
With violets shrinking — and roses rife —
 And fairies could live at the bottom of it."

So I made my way to a certain store
 That flatters susceptible flower growers —
Bought the latest wrinkle in tools for seeding
And squirts that sprinkle, and forks for weeding,
 A label and stake for every flower,
 A fertilizer of evident power
And rakes and rollers, and barrows and mowers.

A reeling and writhing garden hose,
 A kneeling pillow (some clerk put that in),
A spray that reduces botanical vermin
And gadgets whose uses I couldn't determine.
 And I scattered assorted bulbs among
 Some potted plants, in an unknown tongue,
All Greek to me, but possibly Latin.

And I sent them home to my gardening wife,
 Who spaded and troweled each workable minute.
Come visit my garden, the pride of my life,
 It's worth every bit of the thought I put in it.

"Of course Mrs Aaron Ward used to be the rose"

I VISIT MY FIRST GARDEN

(A young girl gets her first glimpse of horticulture. With necessary explanatory notes.)

It was with trepidation that I listened to the message, "Mrs. Vander Tassel is in the Garden and would be pleased to have you come out." My first Garden! ! With expectation I followed the maid toward the French windows leading to the terrace. Should I escape while I could? There was still time to turn and flee. But curiosity plucked at my sleeve and I stepped out.

I located my hostess because of her protective coloring. Had she dressed attractively she might have merged into the floral background, and, as I learned afterward, might have been sprayed, sprinkled or pruned. So as a safeguard she wore an intriguing costume consisting of a hat brimful of floppiness and seagoing slacks with a fore-and-aft rig. She was kneeling, facing away from me, and seemed completely surrounded by numberless surgical instruments and baskets, both mechanized and immobile.

(NOTE 1: The National Association of Manufacturers of Garden Gadgets has estimated that five hundred new implements are put on the market each year. They claim this has been going on since Adam invented the slogan: "An apple a day keeps the doctor away," in opposing any repetition of the intercostal operation which gave him a tireless Eve

"They may come up for Macy's, but they won't
come up for me."

and many stupid afternoons while she worked in the Garden. All of these tools do nothing but scratch, cut or dig holes but they keep steel from going into useless objects such as skyscrapers, battleships and paper clips.)

She finally saw me, cracked an earthy smile in my direction and waved an oversize and over-dirty glove at me.

"My dear," she called, "Why didn't you come last week when my Anthony Waterer was so gorgeous?"

(NOTE II: Gardens are always in the past or in the future.)

I hopscotched down the broken flag walk toward her.

(NOTE III: Disrespect for the flag is flagrant in the better Gardens. It is not considered sporting to lay the flagstones either square or flat. They must be fractured into odd-shaped splinters and fitted together with enough space between them to make tripping easy. Mean little flowers grow, whisker-like, in the cracks, thus combining physical ankle-spraining with mental hedge-hopping.)

There I was in a Garden at last. But I discovered, to my embarrassment, that a Garden is really a small stadium. All about the edges the flowers are arranged in tiers with tall ones standing up in the back and little ones lying down in front. And they all stare at you. Unless you are used to being stared at you develop a sort of claustrophobia. I poked a finger at something

33

and said: "Oh, I like that!!" Mrs. Vander Tassel un-jackknifed herself erect and seemed pleased. She said, "Yes, I've been very lucky with my President Hoover."

(NOTE IV: The proper rejoinder to Mrs. Vander T.'s remark should be, "And I'm having capital success with my Souvenir de Claudius Pernet, Mrs. Erskine Pembroke Thom and Gruss an Teplitz." But the real effect of Mrs. Vander T.'s remark was to indicate that she was a Fourth-and-Highest-Degree Gardener. The other degrees speak as follows:
First Degree (Not admitted to Garden Clubs):
"Say, Joey, got any flowers in your back yard?" "Sure, pansies, hollyhocks, bachelor buttons, marigolds. Go in and pick yourself a bunch." Imagine picking a flower in a Garden!!
Second Degree (The Greeks and Romans had a word for it.)
"Is your Antirrhinum in bloom yet, Doris?"
"Yes, Kendall, but my Lychnis, Lythrum, Matthiola, Matricaria and Mesembryanthum are lousy. They're over behind these bushes." Tut! Tut! Doris, there never are "Bushes" in a Garden, the proper and polite name is "Shrub."
Third Degree (Intimate first-name conversation. Listen to these phlox-phanciers.)
"Audrey, how was your subulata?"
"Fine, Aubrey, and your divaricata—"
"Profuse, and your suffruticosa"—
"As nice as your cuspidata—"
"And your decussata, Audrey, don't forget—"
"I was really thinking of your paniculata—"
Both together: "After all it's only Drummondi that we have any real luck with."
Fourth Degree (Almost incomprehensible)
"Yes, Professor, Black Knight got black spot; but I still have Lancelot who goes well with Guinevere in the perennial bed, and you, Claire—"
"My elegans alba grandiflora will not amount to much this year but wait till you see my speciosum magnificum and auratum platyphyllum—")

34

Mrs. Vander Tassel left her ironmongery and showed me about. "You have a lovely Garden here," I said.

"My dear," she replied, "this is only ONE of my Gardens. This next," as we ducked through a pergola, "is my Hyphenate Garden. Here's where I have 'Love-lies-bleeding,' 'Devil-in-the-bush,' 'Snow-on-the-mountain,' 'Cup-and-saucer-Bells,' 'Forget-me-nots,' 'Johnny-jump-ups,' and 'Red-hot-pokers.' I dig a few punctuation marks into the soil and it gets results. And here is my Weed Garden. I give the happy little fellows a playground of their own and they never bother the other Gardens at all." She squeezed through a rustic gate.

"Here's a useful Garden. I call it my Mirror-up-to-Nature Garden. I put a looking-glass on one side of a seedling and its picture from the seed catalog on the other. It positively prevents shirking. Then I've got a Black Garden — can't be seen at all at night."

"And what's this strange Garden?" I asked, stopping before a crooked stile.

"That's my Rolling Stone Garden. Everything moves. All the rocks in the rock garden turn when you walk on them, and the flowers are all ramblers, climbers and creepers. The little bridges collapse when you step on them, the waterfalls and geysers are piped and

35

squirt at you, the gazing ball makes you look thin, the sundials are set on daylight time, the bird baths have hot and cold running water, and the dish pan pools have alligators in them which snap at you. You see it's a mixture of a Maze and a Mess. But this last new one is my pet —"

"What is it?" I asked, dully.

"It's a Walter Winchell Garden. I only grow in it things that are mentioned in his column."

Lifting my nose I could catch the familiar fragrance of scallions.

(NOTE V: This is the proper time to go home.)

"You can see my problem; there's no mystery."

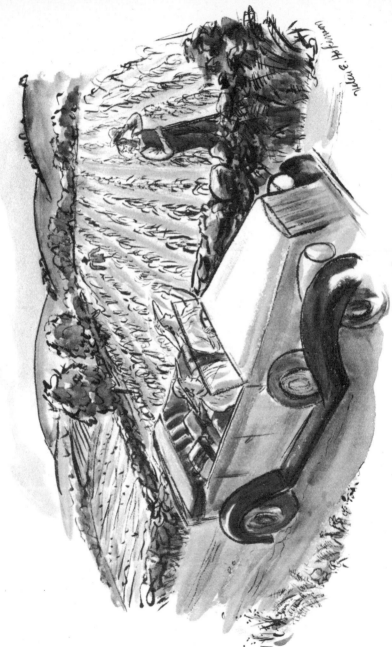

" Are we very far from civilization "

SONG TO MY LOVE

(A poet writes in the language of wild flowers)

The Viper's Bugloss beckons me
  Across the flowery lea,
And a glorious stretch of blue Cow Vetch,
  (Where the Skunk Cabbage used to be).
Where the Devil's Paintbrush nestles,
  And the Harebells sadly peal,
I'll send to my love an armful of
  Hardhack and False Solomon's Seal.

CHORUS
My Sneezeweed, my Chickweed, Joe-Pye Weed,
  My Milkweed, My Ragweed (Achoo! !),
My Fireweed, Ironweed, Jewelweed
(Say you'll be my cruel little Jewelweed),
  Each flower reminds me of you.

The Dutchman's Breeches call to me,
  The Corn Cockles guide my way,
And I'll seek me a bed of Turtlehead
  Where the Corpse Plant holds it sway.
Where the Toadflax sports with the Goat's Rue
  And the bees round the Cow Lilies hum,
My spirits feed on Rattlesnake Weed,
  As I wait for my love to come.

CHORUS
My Moneywort, Liverwort, Soapwort,
  My Stitchwort, My Toothwort, my child,
My Spiderwort, Mitrewort, Motherwort,
(My dear little, queer little Motherwort),
  The flowers are driving me wild.

39

"We're sorry about the petunias."

DOGS IN A CITY GARDEN

To you, Blitzen, and you, Donner,
   Of the Ancient Tribe of Teckel,
God has given you the honor
   To protect, to love, to heckle.

To patrol the green environs,
   To insult the passing throng,
And to answer fire sirens
   With a melancholy song.

Boys on bicycles and postmen
   Must be dealt with unafraid,
You have braver hearts than most men,
   Softer eyes than any maid.

Slipper-chewer, candy-cadger,
   Actors in a dozen roles,
Will you ever find a badger
   In those inconvenient holes?

Tree inspector, border ranger,
   Knock-knees over wide spread feet,
Hurtling valiant into danger,
   Never signalling defeat.

Forehead furrowed deep with worry,
   Duty keeps you sorely tried,
Till like doughnuts, red and furry,
   You are dozing at my side.

Those who laugh at your dimensions,
   Long of tail and short of limb,
Suffer strange miscomprehensions
   Of your strength of will and whim.

Let the foxhound and the fox hunt
   Interest some men of station,
Give me gardens and a dachshund
   As a daily occupation.

"Just give me a waterfall, and I'm the happiest woman in the world."

WHERE ARE YOU GOING TO SIT?

God has given us arms and ankles,
    Muscles and brains and wit
And God has furnished a very superior
Properly placed and padded posterior
    Whereupon we can sit.
God has given us yielding meadows,
    Velvety spreads of lawn,
Pine needles, moss, and resilient grasses
For sensible lads and sensible lasses
    To rest these posteriors on.

But man has discovered such things outdated,
    Meager in eye-appeal,
Calls for furniture chromium-plated,
    Fashioned of structural steel.

Flexible tubes with a strange, uncanny,
    Catapult sense of grip,
That curve their tentacles round your fanny
    And seize your reluctant hip.

"*Doesn't* anything *rock* any more?"

Leather contraptions which never *will* work;
    Castings, of durable line,
Leave you impressed with their lovely grille-work,
    As well as a waffle design.

Mushrooms of metal which softly bounce you;
    Marble, which leaves you cold,
And wooden crates which may soon renounce you,
    And many a tail unfold.

Corduroy seats of impassioned rubber
    To tickle you round on round,
And comfort the diligent digger and grubber,
    But not fundamentally sound.

Reed and rattan which determined schemers
    Make to untwist on the spot
With sharp little nails to impale your femurs
    And rip where you'd just rather not.

Chairs heavy-footed of ponderous iron
    Settling knee-deep in the mud,
And canvas things which you lie, and rely on
    Which let you down with a thud.

Terrible troughs which a child can wangle
    With ease from some pieces of pine
That leave you bent in a sharp right-angle,
    A permanent crimp in your spine.

Concrete stretchers which chill your marrow,
    Hassocks, eternally damp,
Benches to trundle about like a barrow—
    If you are the heavyweight champ.

God made men and God made monkeys
    And most of the latter are found with
A curly, strong and very prehensile
Tail, which they find is a swell utensil
    Simply for hanging around with.
But men, though descended from apes and tree-tops
    And called an intelligent gang,
Since all of these years they have never hit on
A garden seat which is safe to sit on
    Might better, like monkeys, go hang.

"Are you our host?"

A garden hose in its original state may be defined as a small body of water completely surrounded by rubber. The game consists in trying to keep most of the water inside the rubber and, if it does get out, of guessing where it is going to go. To start properly all you need is the hose and the small body of water. Clothes do not matter, in fact, the less there are of them the less they matter.

Go to the nearest hose store and buy a length of hose. Always be sure that the hose is considerably shorter than the garden. This saves a lot of reeling around and it gives one practice in high-angle fire on the bunch of hollyhocks which are just out of range against the farthest fence.

If you get the right kind of hose it will have a muzzle, or nozzle, on one end, and a funny doohickey on the other that turns around and around. Be careful to specify garden hose and do not pick up what is known as gas tubing. This latter is used only for suicides, and you will not need it immediately.

Instead of selling you a diver's costume for protection, the hose salesfellow will now try to interest you in a hose-reel. This is a sort of hose baby carriage which protects it when resting and allows you to get it back

5o

in its stall without dragging most of the garden and the garden bench with you.

Having got the hose and the hose-reel, you now have the choice of tooling it home through traffic or having it sent. That is for you to decide.

In your imagination you picture the happy husband and garden-lover hosing his garden. A smiling wife stands beside him while about him play the innocent children. It is just as well to keep this picture in your mind as you hose. Anywhere else it would get awfully wet.

We will assume that in the course of time the hose and reel arrive and are put into the garden. First find a hose-bib. This is not what you think it is or what it ought to be, but is merely a name for a spigot to fasten the incoming end of the hose to. In the modern house it is out under the living-room window in the center of a nettle patch. In the older houses it is at the kitchen sink, and the hose has to be threaded through the kitchen, the furnace room, the pantry, and the laundry. This usually leaves just enough on the outside of the house to allow you, with your back against the wall, to shoot from the hip.

Take the doohickey on the end of the hose and try to fasten it to the faucet (hose-bib). After some reluctance it will set its front teeth in it and hold on. Turn

"We've been so fortunate. We've always had a thrush."

on the water full force. The hose will let go with a guzzling sound, and the water will run into your shoes. Turn off the water and try again. Be patient. In time the mandibles will grip and hold the hose. As soon as this happens turn on the water again. If the hose is working, the water will gush out the nozzle and through the open dining-room window. Grab the hose by the neck just behind the ears and twist the muzzle. It will desist after a struggle in which your collar is soaked.

You are now prepared to assume the easy and artless position of garden hoser which you have looked forward to. Take a natural position — one hand in your trousers pocket, light your pipe, hold the hose dangling in one hand, and turn the nozzle. Immediately a stream of water will burst forth and wash the hat off a fond neighbor, who is passing at that moment on the other side of the fence. Disappear behind the nearest shrub and turn the nozzle the other way. You will now find yourself in the center of a small amateur shower bath. Show yourself to be master and ride your hose until it calms down. Remember a hose always knows who is driving it and never forgets an unkindness.

In time you will be able to do all sorts of fanciful things with the little plaything. By waving the muzzle back and forth rapidly you can make the most intriguing watery snakes that eventually will wash away all the nasturtiums. By pointing the hose directly into the air, you can imitate a summer rainstorm beautifully until your wife, who is behind the grape arbor (and directly in the line of fire), tells you to stop or she will take it away from you. Then again you can aim at certain plants and see how near you can hit them either by direct fire straight ahead or by surprising them by a sort of anti-aircraft attack over the spirea bushes.

From time to time the water will stop running for no apparent reason. After long investigation it has been found that this fading, so-called, is due to any or all of the following reasons:

(1) The city reservoir has run dry.

(2) You have not paid your water taxes, and the city has tried to take it out on your garden in a mean way.

(3) Some unnecessarily cleanly person has decided to take a bath.

(4) Some dirty crook has turned off the tap (hose-bib).

(5) The doohickey has lost its bulldog grip and has fainted in the performance of its duty.

(6) You have a puncture, blowout, or arterial hemorrhage somewhere in the hose itself.

(7) The hose in a fit of insanity has wound itself

around the pedestal of the bird bath and its windpipe is shut off.

(8) You are standing on it.

This leads one to the opposite emergency: when you want to shut off the hose. The natural way is to twist the trachea of the hose until it stops. Which direction this is, is not generally known in advance. From my own experience I have noted the following sequence of spasms from twisting the nozzle: long needle jet, wide fuzzy spray, which gets less and less until it becomes long drippy spout and then a wide-angle rainstorm. After this the muzzle comes off in your hand and the water runs out quite naturally and up your coat sleeves, if you have been foolish enough to wear a coat.

Another method is to spring on the hose suddenly when it is facing the other way and twist it into a loop. To do this one must let go its neck and, as soon as the hose knows about it, it will turn on you suddenly and vent its spleen down your shirt, if you have been silly enough to have one on.

After you have sprayed, sprinkled, and inundated a portion of the garden and are standing up to the differential in water the wanderlust moves you to parts yet unwashed. When you have progressed ten feet a slight tugging will cause you to turn about and discover that the hose has cut a circular swath through the delphinium and snapdragons, tipped over the watering can and some potted plants, and is now about to overturn the gazing ball. Also the penstock (hose-bib) has been bent into a strangely inquiring expression.

All good fun must come to an end and after a while you decide that you are wet enough and it is time to stop. Go to the water-cock (hose-bib) and turn off the stream. You are now ready to reel up your hose on your hose-reel.

On looking over this piece of automotive equipment you will find a sort of device to catch the doohickey at the inhaling end of the hose. It is now a simple matter to wind up the creature on the spool. You will find at this point that the hose has become completely waterlogged and has absorbed twice its own capacity of water. It squirts this out in a reluctant way as it worms toward you along the ground, keeping the last two quarts to empty into the cuffs of your trousers if you are insane enough to be still wearing them. After this final outburst the hose will remain quite quiet, and you may gently roll it back to its parking space in the garage. You have done your bit; you have hosed the garden, and you enter into the warmth of your home, a good deed well done. Half an hour later a thunderstorm breaks overhead and it rains continuously for five hours.

"Mr. Beal is noted for his fearless treatment of rock gardens."

Rub-a-dub-dub,
The men and the grub
Are fighting it out over flower and shrub,
The butchers, the bakers,
The candlestick makers
Are suddenly turned into hoers and rakers;
And down on their knees in a common belief
Are Richman and Poorman and Beggar and Thief.

Barton the Banker is out in his tweeds
Wheedling a seedling, impeding the weeds,
Tooling an edger
Forgetful of ledger,
Far from financing industrial needs.
Is this the man who a moment ago
Looked at you boldly and coldly said "No"?
Is this the one — why it's quite unbelievable —
Frowned at Bills Payable, doubted Receivable?—
Look at him now gladly lending an ear
And learning of pruning, authentic and clear.
Who is the expert that he must kowtow to?
Why, Benny the Beggar is showing him how to.

Benny the Beggar has blossoms galore,
Hyacinth, hollyhock, myrtle and more,
What if the neighbors,
Describing his labors
Laugh at his foxglove and wolf at the door!
Simple his tools are and leaky his hose is
But nobody knows how he raises such roses.
Rain does his spraying, the snow fertilizes,
A touch of his hand and his stock simply rises,
What does he care if the mortgage is due?
He has his mint and his marigold, too.
But where is he getting advice about canker,
And fungus, and flies? Why, from Barton the Banker.

Hi! dibble-dibble
The water-pots dribble,
The gardeners dig and the editors scribble.
It's catalog time
And dammit if I'm
Not carried away by a nursery rhyme.
So put on your sneakers, your dirtiest pants,
And get out, you sluggards, and go to the ants.

"You can't trust them, they spread."

BY ANY OTHER NAME

The flower beds of Esther
   Are beautiful by nature
Yet how I do detest her
   Obnoxious nomenclature
For Leopard's bane and Loosestrife
   And Feverfew and Spurge
Incite the heart to new strife
   And kill the vernal urge.

And with pedantic Phyllis
   There's nothing that she misses
Each yellow Daffodil is
   A species of Narcissus;
The learning she discloses
   Is lost on simple me,
That which I call a rose, is
   To her a "Hybrid Tea."

So when it's all debated
   It's Lila heads my list,
She's not been designated
   A horticulturist.
Her lawn is full of hummocks
   But it's a place we can
Lie flat upon our stomachs
   And get the swellest tan.

"She's hog-wild today. She's going to transplant all the petunias."

FINAL WARNING

You who start upon a garden
  Implements all new and nice,
May I offer, with your pardon,
  Unsolicited advice:

Know, as waiting at the portal
  With your fancy taking wings,
That the only things immortal
  Are magenta-colored things;

Though you battle with insistence
  Aphids, beetles, bugs and ants,
That these creatures' whole existence
  Lies in eating up your plants;

That each floral new creation,
  Feeling it is truly great,
Needs a special invitation —
  Only weeds will crash the gate;

That no garden gives enjoyment
  Howsoever well begun
Where you cannot give employment
  To the Firm of Rain & Sun.

Learn your lore in sheltered cloisters
  Letter-perfect to a fault
But if gardens are your oysters,
  Take them with a grain of salt.

Keep this mental food, well seasoned,
  But the conquest always comes
To the one with iron knees, and
  Indefatigable thumbs.